TRAVELING

ALSO BY PAUL VANGELISTI

Just in Time (Fruita, CO: Lithic Press, 2024)
Fragment Science: Tecnici del Bianco (with William Xerra; Milan:
    Edizioni il verri, 2023)
Liquid Prisoner (Lithic Press, 2021).
Motive and Opportunity (Bristol: Shearsman Books, 2020)
Imperfect Music (Modena: Edizioni Galleria Mazzoli, 2019)
Toodle-oo (Los Angeles / Bagnone: Magra Books, 2017)
Border Music (Greenfield, MA: Talisman House, 2016)
Solitude (Modena: Edizioni Mazzoli, 2015)
Six White Mules / Sei muli bianchi (Milano: Edizioni del Verri, 2014)
Wholly Falsetto with People Dancing (Los Angeles: Seismicity Eds, 2013)
Mapping Stone (with Dennis Phillips, Milano / Los Angeles: postmedia
    books / Seismicity Editions, 2013)
Two (Greenfield, MA: Talisman House, 2010)
Azusa: a Sequel (Los Angeles: Pie In The Sky Press, 2009)
La vita semplice / A Simple Life (Modena: Galleria Mazzoli, 2009)
Alphabet 2007 / Alfabeto 2007 (Modena: Galleria Mazzoli, 2007)
Days Shadows Pass (Los Angeles: Green Integer, 2006)
Caper (2 vols., with Ray DiPalma, Piacenza: ML & NLF, 2006)
Agency (Los Angeles: Seeing Eye Books, 2003)
Embarrassment of Survival: Selected Poems, 1970–2000 (New York:
    Marsilio / Agincourt Editions, 2001)
Alphabets (Los Angeles: Littoral Books, 1999)
A Life (Piacenza: ML & NLF, 1997)
Luci e colori d'Italia (Mantova: Corradini Editore, 1996)
Nemo (Los Angeles: Sun & Moon Books, 1995)
The Simple Life (Modena: Lab. d'Arte Grafica Roberto Gatti, 1993)
Villa (Littoral Books, 1991)
Rime (Red Hill Press, 1983)
Another You (Red Hill, 1981)
Un grammo d'oro (Rome: Cervo Volante, 1981)
Portfolio (Los Angeles & Fairfax, CA: Red Hill, 1978)
Remembering the Movies (Red Hill, 1977)
2 x 2 (Red Hill, 1977)
La stanza stravagante (Turin: Edizioni Geiger, 1976)
The Extravagant Room (Red Hill Press, 1976)
Pearl Harbor (San Francisco: Isthmus Press, 1975)
Il tenero continente (Turin: Edizioni Geiger, 1975)
The Tender Continent (Los Angeles: Chatterton's Bookstore, 1974)
Air (Red Hill Press, 1973)
Communion (Fairfax, CA: Red Hill, 1970)

Paul Vangelisti

TRAVELING

Shearsman Books

First published in the United Kingdom in 2025 by
Shearsman Books Ltd
PO Box 4239
Swindon
SN3 9FN

Shearsman Books Ltd Registered Office
30–31 St. James Place, Mangotsfield, Bristol BS16 9JB
(this address not for correspondence)

www.shearsman.com

EU AUTHORISED REPRESENTATIVE:
Lightning Source France
1 Av. Johannes Gutenberg, 78310 Maurepas, France
Email: compliance@lightningsource.fr

ISBN 978-1-84861-984-5

CONTENTS

And the cunning animals immediately
notice the world's a language in which
we're not always quite at home.
—Rainer Maria Rilke

The fields say to me: stream
and the streams to me: fields?
—René Char

Exteriors

A THREAD OF HOPE

Here there, a rhythm behind the moon
and her six white mules aspiring.
Is it all rhyme at this age
or more like a clock on the mantelpiece
shedding the hours, mirror above
the bathroom sink washing hands?

*

Dream of dinner and drinks with Ray in North Beach.
Hop a cab on West Side Highway and drive back,
top down, the air whistling over our heads.
Glad to be showing him my city,
a few spots maybe missed back when.
Splurge on clams, mussels, crab and three desserts.

*

But just a dream after all –
Upper Westside and North Beach
a short drive from each other.
Almost four years now Ray's been gone.
Glad to be thinking about dessert
and forget what floor the car's on.
Who's stepping through the mirror?
Yesterday was the first day of summer.

*

Like Pound's *rushlight* in pine wood
or in some great colonnade.
The eye spying a melody
among rows of skinny palms at mind's end
and numberless blue. In this lewd
province a thread of hope.

*

Who fashioned hell, made suffering
of us, by us, for us?
Embarrassment pervading chaos,
a dwindling presence squandering
even its own son. Who made us?
The devil made us.

*

And what 'unfinished' means?
That one keeps at it?
In mind's eye unable to fall asleep,
stumbling giddily out of bed
to scribble in another room?
Undone, unnecessarily?

*

The blank page not so much
a daunting or finish
but the emptiness behind me,
thread of a past unraveling
daily. Or darkness
about to come morning.

*

These lines fresh from nothing to do
on a much too sunny Sunday,
the end or start of a week.
Waiting for the afternoon to cool
and more than someplace to go:
six verses framing a porch in shade.

*

The rash figure of an old man
with silence at the bone.
And what about the rest of the day,
so little now steals into the poem
as once garbage trucks or crows
or even the March wind in love.

ALMOST DANCING

The top down, south on Orange Grove,
shimmering rendition of stucco
and gain. Life by any other name,
never too far from roving words
and their silences. A slight footing
to begin with, one after the other
like palms along the boulevard.

*

The bright foot in time now reduced
to metaphor as we are to illness.
In Italy under strict quarantine,
people sing out from their balconies
to their beloved cities. *Vox populi.*
Invoking that ancient trust in the voice
risen above the earth to airy nothing.

*

To grab them by the throat with your joy,
sang Pagliarani too many years ago.
With a sky like this, sunlight and dark clouds,
a letting-go for all those girls and boys
who gave it all away. Why now a blueprint
one seems never to have wanted? Is it age
or the plain stubbornness of carrying on?
And a flock of pigeons in this brilliant
veering gray, then silver then gray again.
As below the high cloud and the hill,
a rush of leave-taking or arrival
who can know exactly what or when?

*

The palm's hardly 'at the end of the mind'
but outside my second-floor window.
Today the heads on the screen speak
of isolation as the 'new normal.'
In the lift of a foot, fronds and pink stucco
and the gliding, as I stare at the palm
waiting for some creature to light on it.

HERE THERE
for Ray DiPalma, in memoriam

Though hardly the jeweled steps of Dioce,
the faded stucco climb in warming light,
ascending from the trash bins,
from the late night you just had to know
how the crime unfolded, who confessed,
what clues you overlooked all along.

*

Though not so much a color
as an indifferent quiet
absorbing a flock of parrots
into ordinary blue.
Maybe something of a cloud
one has often imagined
in the corner of a window.

*

Figuring thought sometimes futile
as flipping the notebook pages
after a simple phrase
misplaced upon waking.
Here there, an envelope harboring
what's left behind, remaining
unsealed, maybe unnamed
and back on a bottom shelf.
Here there, a way to thinking
out this window in morning light.

ANOTHER DANCE

I won't dance, don't ask me
I won't dance, don't ask me to.
So what's on for today?
Besides dragging myself out of bed
to make coffee, wash a few glasses
and start cleaning and chopping vegetables
for a week's pot of chicken soup?
Not ready for Sybille Bedford's memoir,
Quicksands, or the last of McKinty's
Forsyth novels, or rereading
Vattimo's *Beyond Interpretation.*
Maybe a green sauce for the chicken,
though must shop for fresh parsley
and on the way back swing by the P.O.
to ship some calendars up north.
And after lunch rouse enough ire
to call AT&T and demand
an end to our never-ending robot calls.
And most likely time for a car wash
(senior discount Wednesday)
and then back home before 5
for a nice long walk along the Arroyo.

UNION & COLUMBUS
for Giulia Niccolai

Deliberately breathes patience
exhaling impatiently.
A zero sum of white, a blank.
Once upon a time printers employed
technicians of whitespace to allow
for eternity's lie on the page.
Breathless and emptier than speech,
the poem hollows out a space
where there's no more space.

The quiet at dusk carries downstream.
Canyon light stray as a melody
outside the second-story window
of a strange room on a strange corner
where I never lived as a boy.

A THOUGHT

for Neeli Cherkovski

Not exactly private, your personal library
maps an attitude to the world, even if the word's
increasingly difficult these days. Almost difficult
as 'beauty,' if that kind of failure remains possible.
Most conspiracies of some toying with their devices,
preferring not to handle a book, flip pages, to read
or to be read by letters and sounds that overwhelm us.
The path through the forest discovers a dizzying place,
a clearing reached after many years among words
that some mornings are unfamiliar as one's middle name.
A library where public and personal correspond,
when thoughts and a desire to scribble more or less
coincide. The clearing's gone, the book's back on the shelf,
and another book there on the armchair overnight.

Or the jovial reply of our 96-year-old neighbor just
encountered at the mailboxes:
"I'm doing well, I think." Defining with her gallant smile, a
time when understanding seems a luxury reserved for the very
rich or the very intolerant.

Waking below the glowing shutter
birdsong suspended in the glare.
To shuffle the hallway's length
in dazzled hush, spoon out coffee
recalling a favorite title on the shelves,
now lost, like much else, to sleep.

.

GOOD MORNING

Once the pen starts over the page,
all's an afterthought to lingering.
Goodbye, goodbye, misplaced dreams.
Today must be shorter than yesterday,
easier and probably less finicky
than tomorrow. Hello, unknowing,
you must be somebody's lovely daughter.

*

Just an ordinary wilderness.
Everybody and the birds quiet,
not a critter astir in the overcast.
What to make of a plea for oblivion,
a passage one could as easily skip?
Car door out front, then a rumbling start.
Today's about ready to begin.

*

To listen to what one doesn't know,
while sunlight plays across the eucalyptus,
through creamy louvers onto the marble
tabletop. A sound you've not heard, where
you haven't been. "One more time," the Count calls
to his orchestra at the end of
"April in Paris." And then again
a final invitation: "One more once."

*

Autumn's here, colors keener in the wind:
green sways varying shades, a wedge of blue
above the rooftiles and this easiest urge
to step out and feel skin meeting light.
Light rousing in these failing eyes,
and more light upholding morning.

*

Overcast remains and parrot shrieking
of an early Saturday morning. How such
unlovely sound in locating oneself?
A drift north, remote as childhood, or maybe
just maundering before what's to follow.
Almost wrote *fallow*, as with welcome
silences in a courtyard of palms.

*

Tempting to upend the morning's course.
Curse? "Style is death," exclaimed the poet
in a more optimistic time. The top down,
noon flimsy as tissue streaming past.
West on Beverly, east on Beverly.

*

Early November night in Pasadena.
Staring at flood-lit palms you think, why here?
Besides, the lighting isn't that important
or the location, even the script.
Surely not at this age or time of day.
To the littlest words: good morning.

WETTING A LINE

It's hard to imagine a simpler life, dreaming
he's at his old job even if little is the same.
He must explain what he's doing there and it's not easy
to make people understand. Sometimes he's overcome
by a need to sleep, especially in the mornings.
At breakfast he confesses to his wife that his colleagues
appear less and less educated and often ill-prepared,
but then what does he know? He likes staying up late
reading, nodding off now and then in his easy chair,
avoiding the grinning faces that fill his nights.
If the water wouldn't be too low, he might try fishing
the San Gabriel tomorrow, if he didn't have to leave
so early to beat the traffic. Maybe a late start,
even if it means working the riffles a little harder.
He would like to abandon himself to the river
upstream along the west side of the canyon.

THE SIMPLE LIFE (alternate take)

No news is good news was the motto
when working in the newsroom
in my late twenties. Now staring out
at the lush fields after a shower,
breeze tripping among the grapevines
and poplars, not at all sure what we meant.
Surely tired of the furious deadlines,
with judging the import of events
to be forgotten in a year or so,
annoyed with having to get it right
in the simplest and least words possible.

The wind's almost stopped, cicadas back
to a steady chorus, the sun crawling
through the door flickers in the treetops.
Some fifty years ago, never time
in those eager days to consider
this hillside, allowing the heat
to open before me like a book,
lost and found and lost again.

BEGINNING TO SEE THE LIGHT

Sleeplessness, as you like, means nothing,
loss the object of your desiring,
wind at the bone, alone and a breath away.
Why step back from our 'sedentary trade'?
Maybe the impatience of aging,
the tedium of disciplined days,
simple, inconclusive beginnings.
A little late for the primitive
and likely worn-out for the naïve.
Imitation surely less flattering than
self-defense, despite rainbows in my wine.
A poverty of imagination,
compassion, etc., whatever missing
or just lacking a home. Desire
remains unfortunately serious,
at least serious enough to dismiss.
Come along, your lips burning close mine.

Traveling

Caro Andrea,

Scrivo in inglese perché rimane la lingua dei miei dubbi. Each night for the last week or so, I go to bed comfortable in my doubts. I'm retired (that's the term) from profession or career. I've been to most of these places before, or at least I'm under that impression.

So I travel in what aren't exactly reveries, a modest ambling, if you will, with floppy hat and hands behind my back, peering here and there, noting whatever of interest. The object of my travel doesn't seem so important at this age as much as the sheer adventure of it. Echoing the words of the immortal Yogi Berra, when you come to a fork in the road, take it.

I travel not so much intent on destination, more interested in the method or measure of travel. Whom do I meet, why bother to speak to me? Most of the places look familiar enough, houses, trees, bushes and avenues. Birds and dogs seem happy and always welcome. Traffic's another matter, though generally I'm not so much aware of it in sleep.

*

Are you still at the window,
a different tune, a lesser moon
to answer? Music ever listens
to search your verses that search
and scribble you. Who is there
and here you are although why
must you assume a prior slip
from this room into the dark?

A conversation overheard about how
the page always lies between us
heeding this heedless purpose.
And each morning one gets up
as the day's front to back
back to front freshly enough.

*

Who wouldn't at least abandon
your seat at the desk and soar
among the treetops, nodding
to the ravens, saluting
the morning traffic along the boulevard?
Who wouldn't dare the shimmering glass
for faces looking up from coffee
and newspapers, bills and notices
pushed away to another day?
Or maybe simply hover
in dizzy flight above the pages?

*

Being a few seconds or a lifetime
before the turn in the stair and feet
tumbling downstairs to the outside door.

Whether afternoons or winters,
leaves underfoot along the sidewalk
to the first corner passing trees.

Turning over the pillow and wondering
how long to morning's glimmer
and listening much of one's life.

*

I've come to see travel as a form of speculation or, perhaps better,
that speculating's become a favorite mode of travel. Can't help
but recall the fabled exchange between Emerson and Thoreau.
Emerson, that grand Yankee expansionist mind, calling into
question his friend's habit of not venturing beyond his (Thoreau's)
native Concord. Thoreau's blithe rejoinder, that he travels
extensively in Concord, seems very much to the point.

*

Mind takes well enough to travel well,
mostly a matter of what's left behind.
A palm stands outside the window
as does one just outside the door
of our house in Italy.
Desk and chair sit on the top floor
of both houses. As there too,
the more I scribble the more I begin
nodding off weary of myself.
Here as there, all my dear dead
will soon be preparing lunch,
keeping an eye on the broccoli,
starting up the pasta water,
making sure the oil doesn't overheat.

*

Packing, even a suitcase
holds anxiety. Can't wait to unpack
no matter how late arriving.
Prefer not to be reminded
of being away. The idea,
rather than the thing itself,
perhaps more hospitable.

Am I, as in my earliest years,
unnerved by experience,
and now toward the end of life
spooked by the pitch of the physical.
Questions feel improbable
as answers, and more often
omitting question marks like these.

*

Dichtung = *condensare,*
Uncle Ez insisted of this adventure,
meaning cut and cut again
until one risks that gravest sin of aging:
omission. Notwithstanding its own
operative humor, omitting
what must soon be omitted,
dozing off for a moment
into the sweetest of omissions.

*

I dreamed of sitting so vividly
couldn't wait to wake up and sit.
Sometimes I speak to my wife,
a few strangers and to you.
I sit and listen to the rain,
an occasional gust shaking the palm
and then a comfortable silence.
Perhaps I've broken my leg,
though there isn't any pain
sitting here until first light.
The phone rings almost waking
and a familiar voice reminds
it's my own voice droning on.

*

Centuries ago *terra incognita* mapped somewhere one didn't know and thus could scarcely imagine. Memory – not sure how it is with you – seems impossibly tangled. Or put another way, one loses oneself imagining what one can't remember, and vice versa. Isn't memory, or at least mine, an unimaginable place of shifting borders? Today she wore a red dress and sandals, yesterday she was from Milwaukee and loved oysters, while tomorrow remains, as Bob wrote, "a wicked place to start remembering things."

*

Sometimes talking with you leaves me tongue-tied, seeming to eavesdrop at best on our conversation. Words and phrases feel vertiginous, though nonetheless attractive, even if there's an uneasy sense of puttering around out of my depth. In essence, you cause me to reconsider, often relish what I'm about to say, and say it, unfortunately as one will. I enjoy our chats, pointless as they must at times seem to you. Caught between memory and imagination, trapped between languages here and there. Toodle-oo.

*

Having not heard from him since December, Nanni Cagnone
called to let me know he was doing better after a pretty serious
fall. What apparently turned things around for him, banishing
a delirious depression, was sitting down and writing a sequence
of poems – 100 poems in 34 days – which he's planning to call
"Esito"("Outcome"). And which, he added, might turn out to be
his last book of poetry. Toward the end of our conversation, after
I mumbled something about my eye problems and relentless
reading habits, Nanni came back with an aside which made
me think of you. Detective novels sometimes end well, though
philosophy always ends badly.

*

And now just beyond the page
failing a way to sound words
one can't remember, fascinated
with the teasing emptiness.

Dialogo, monologo forse,
you wrote yesterday about this
back and forth. *Logos*, what one knows
and *Lowghost*, as it's called way out west.
The specter or impossibility
left over from an pleasing dream,
a memory lingering just
around the corner as only
a sliver of moon inflects the fancy.

Were you invisible as a boy?
Not so much a confession
but a squeeze of unmade flesh,
who may or may not be singing like us.

*

In the 1933 film we watch the Invisible Man as he opens a door, strolls through a gate down a country lane and laughs out loud. In 1854 on the Tehacipi Ranchero, just west of the Mojave Desert, a couple of vaqueros turn in their saddles to witness the approaching men, women and children, emaciated, hollow-eyed and ghostlike after making it across the wilderness. Having, in their (the survivors') own words, "seen the elephant." Two centuries, two different phantoms; one science fiction, the other a history more improbable than fiction. Exile *to* or exile *from*. What did Brecht write in "On the Term of Exile":

> Don't worry about watering the flowers—
> In fact, don't plant them.
> You will have gone back home before they bloom,
> And who will want them?

*

All night trying to recall the designer of the San Francisco Maritime Museum, convinced he had two same names. The Aquatic Park building was an icon of my youth, a Moderne vessel above the small beach where I caught sand dabs. I haunted the place until my first years of college, walking by on my way to fish, bringing a sandwich to watch the bocce players on the big courts, or just hanging out on the steps below, listening to choruses of African drummers.

Back at my desk memory's indeed a wicked place as the building became the Maritime Museum after the War, first opening in 1941 as a bathhouse for the military. A charming, exotic place, which you and I passed on our walk from the Hyde Street car. The name, evading me throughout the night, was Hilaire Hiler, whose two-story mural, "Sea Hunt," one faces walking in. Ripples of blues and greens floating up the staircase, all sorts of plants and creatures, and pale blue bubbles the size of pumpkins – that aren't, weren't ever there – rising too.

*

Leap year, steep year trivial
as the TV coverage
of who's being born today.
Prisoner to the pioneer,
prisoner to the exception we abuse.
Or maybe just terrified
of the sensational we impose
around the world. As the genius
of the Great Crash of '29,
from the roof of the Empire State,
champagne in hand, proclaimed: "Nothing above,
nothing below, and therefore I leap."

*

"*Notte senza vento.*" Giuliano's new aquatint you presented this past weekend at Gatti's Artesucarte. You associate the glimpse of the Duomo in "Windless Night" with Giuliano's previous book of cathedral prints, *Anima Mania* (1995), for which I did a poem of the same name, and you the translation.

Citing the poem's Italian, you recall the Duomo's many shades of nocturnal blue under which we drank and flourished: *languore di un blu più sospinto* ("longing for what was once a rowdier blue"), as well as a return to *un'altra estate alla mania/ della pienezza*" ("another summer to the mania/for plenty"). Most importantly for me is your reminding of the captivating blues in "windless night," though perhaps no longer dynamic enough for an *anima che sbanda* ("floundering soul"). Perhaps too in "*Notte senza vento*," Giuliano senses that even transformed with age, the memorious night remains ever windless.

*

In *Writing Degree Zero*, Barthes asserts that poetic writing, since Baudelaire, thrives beyond the societal context of writing, that "under each Word in modern poetry there lies a sort of existential geology… the total content of the Name, instead of a chosen content as in classical prose and poetry." The poetic word becomes a Pandora's box from which escape language's potentialities, and a resulting "Hunger of the Word" making…"poetic speech terrible and inhuman," beyond our social norms.

This is partly why I'm so taken with Heidegger's *Four Seminars*, which you recommended during those isolate days of the pandemic, when I spent my time reading philosophy most mornings and detective fiction afternoons and evenings. What most attracted me to Heidegger's talks (as a guest of poet Rene Char's in Provence) is that the philosopher kept returning to *logos* (the reasonable) and its relation to *being*: how, in the Heidegger's words, "logos names being."

As you've noticed, poetry and its lyrical hunger play out in my latest book, "Just in Time." In the piece, "Zig-Zag," a nod to Char himself and to one of my favorite player-composers, Sonny Rollins:

Being, says the old book, brings the river
whispering to the trees that it's all trees
and trees to the river that it's all river.

And later voicing uncertainty in the standard, "Got the World on a String":

The choices grew smaller
and relatively meager,
delighting in words coming together
simply by their outward shape
and music.

*

Logos and detection. *The Gay Science*,
Zarathustra, Parmenides'
fragments, the seventy-five
Inspector Maigrets, from Paris
to New York and back to Paris
after the War. And all the washing
hands, glasses, cups and dishes,
dangling a mask from the left wrist,
at table on sultry parking lot asphalt,
watching traffic cocktail in hand.

Not exactly self-satisfied
more pleasantly occupied,
sufficient, as Malgosia likes to say,
one's eyes shut with traveling.

*

Sorry to hear you were under the weather and hope your trip to Paris is going well. I trust you're enjoying the conference – don't recall the place or subject. I'll check in later this weekend, and thanks for the quote about Nouvelle Vague cinema in 60s Paris and its *traveling halluciné*. Can't wait some nights to close my eyes and be *here there*.

*

Struggled in sleep translating the end of a review – can't recall the language or writer – about an exhibition at a newly opened gallery in New York. Its large spaces were lit up along the avenue like an automotive showroom. I had no idea, nor did the writer, of how to conclude the rambling essay. I wondered how long such a large gallery would stay open with this kind of overhead and relatively new artists. Planned to have drinks with the writer that night and woke about 4a.m relieved there was no such exhibition and no such New York and, above all, nothing for me to do but fall back to sleep with a slight regret, almost a wistfulness for writing that never was.

*

Just out of bed to find your e-mail from Paris: "Today they asked me if there was a relationship between the linear urban structure of Los Angeles and the cinematic technique of *travelling*." Too French and speculative for my taste, the answer demanding a rather unearthly point of view. Besides, *le travelling* in French is the more mundane "dolly" or "tracking shot" here in L.A. Again, the inescapable hallucination of language.

*

Evening walk in breezy light
not unlike beginning this morning.
Happily a mouthful of air
all those years ago and now
imagining who's here there,
easily stepping springtime in place.

As you, dear Neeli, liked to remind
of that second-story window,
now emptier than speech,
across the avenue on the corner
of Union & Columbus,
where I never lived as a boy.

*

In poetry time forever's
another turn of the stair,
a melody lingering
as white daffodils, lavender
and rosemary line the walk,
promise what they will and more
of rhyming into being
that meager, most dubious
river on its course to the sea.
Old Beard sang that same sea
and dew-bejeweled steps of Dioce,
a mounting vision of the forgotten.
"For the blue flash," he repeated,
"and the moments
                    benedetta"

*

What's missing or remembered,
sung or envisioned as it was.
And little more than the desire
to slow gently as a river bend
in sweetest April, a late hatch
provoking cousin trout to the glittering,
and soon shadows mind the canyon walls.

Interiors

RED BONES

Red bones, blue lightening.
how long, how late does it mean?
Without questions are horses possible?
White nights, cold earth, dead water
are the start of what you've always been.
Time's in random turning rhymes
as it will, and rings too often
when you begin to begin again.

Only a few fragments left to shore
and the ruin almost complete
on a windless afternoon.
Neither the palm out my window
nor this reluctant April
leave the mind as it was found.

RIME
for Don

That so many years ago I began,
who can deny a city that gives nothing back,
seems almost routine now and not so dire.
Who can deny the sincerity of
hot dog stands envisioned as hot dogs,
no longer as dizzily arcane
considering the verdict,
who can deny a communion of lovers
at eighty miles per hour shot once through the head.

We did the book at Pat Reagh's shop
near the train station in Glendale.
Rime, a desperately glad adventure,
we thought might never catch up with us,
Atwater, August 1983.

Hail so hard it blanketed lawns
when we began back in May,
and then another stifling summer
we wore easily in those days
before turning forty. A short walk
from where you would settle years later,
just off Glendale Blvd.,
and where in 2019,
as in the poem, you met your end:
to die among strangers once and for all.

So that this May evening cool and gusty
I stroll above the arroyo,
thinking of your quirky smile
and ardent mind and with each step
a pen once meeting the page.

WHISPER

The scent of freshly mowed hillside
filling the doorway, as even
wistfulness glistens in the treetops.
Bird calls repeat what never happens
and mind a way to go on.

Is memory so much hungrier now
for what one did or didn't,
has or hasn't held onto all too briefly
over the years? Little aglitter
in the leaves as birds begin to quiet
with the afternoon threat of rain.

Please concede a simple elegance
to sleep, missing faces, moonlit windows
and your soft whisper of a better world.

DOG EATS MAN
for Dennis Phillips

In Italy in the back room
of a Chinese restaurant
dreaming as always about
teaching poetry. Back and forth
carrying dishes of noodles
talking about abstraction and Plato
and how it's ever *dog-ness eats*
man-ness or *man-ness eats dog-ness,*
and how I couldn't recall Plato scholar
Cornford's first name, though met grandson Adam
in San Francisco.

Waking in Bagnone
adrift in a fifty-year-old poem
just before the final stanza:

> The madman discovered in a book of China's history that
> although words like 'benevolence' and 'righteousness' adorned
> every page, hidden between the lines were the words 'Ch'ih
> jen' {'Eat men'}. ... Don't gossip, warned Mayakovsky before
> his death.

CALIFORNIA
for Luciano

My heart's in play as little else
now at risk. Surely not comfort
or reputation, ease or fancy
or the small hopes of an equally
small winner. I leave as I came
with accumulating doubt
and a flustered, almost clarity
of nothing much to lose. Silence
admits the scratching on notebook pages
this humid July afternoon.
Dozing sounds of evening preparing
and excuses for a California
soon waking to its own cruel summer.

CLOUDS
for Richard

Raggedy clouds and risen moon
lighten my evening stride.
An omen of disquiet
or a kind of bewilderment
lost in everyday wonder,
a connection grown more fragile
than one might easily allow?
Or a doubtful mind most likely
rhyming the morning sheen of
palm fronds outside the window?
Who is there? The end of too many poems
or the beginning of the same
in much different weather.

BARBARIAN

Memories awash in doubt
sliding down the drowsiest pages
empty more or less of intention.
Watching sleep for the next wave
of barbarians and the next.
Waking only at the moment
of recalling a name or a face
though not so often both. Looking
as before we were forgotten,
a much too early morning
listening for another round of tires
mostly north along the boulevard.

SMALL RAIN

Wind condensing color leaves earth
ablaze. Flower butterfly flower
kindling spring. Whether green or else
wind finds you on a hillside misty
with recollection. Small rain
shivers down palm fronds in the breeze.
Too many answers left in sleep.
Too dizzy a day to pretend
like any other. Fresh avocados,
winter promises until April
when you stop counting the years
left to upending easy habits,
simple questions that will keep for now.

ONE MORE TIME

Half-moon again above the South building
just before my 79th year.
Is another place, another life
worth at this point considering?
Uncertainty defines these days,
as difficult to abandon my desk,
the easy chair, books on the shelf
in reading order, even as
September begins to cool
buoyed by the slightest breeze.
Now fully night and the dark
and its few shadows familiar as noon.

GARDENING
for Malgosia

I dream this garden at the heart of things
agleam with hope stolen at first light.
Blessed fog just burning off
as I reach for the car keys
and the business of another day.
Night extending into day and not,
as children fear, day vexing night.
After lunch maybe the promise
of rich coffee at a corner table,
without the dire prospect
of then heading back to work.
The heart's garden, garden's heart
and so little time to remember.

PROMISE

Can't recall the car I drove to work
or fret about finding my way home.
Wandering up and down the lot,
sweaters, shopping bags, sunglasses
on the seats, an umbrella
and pair of slippers on the floor.
Witchcraft and foreboding, don't recognize
any of the interiors.
Morning paper sounds the end of dreams,
the start of reassembling
what desire's undone during the night.
So lighter than air and promises
of finding who you might have been.

MIRROR

English syntax doesn't change easily.
English syntax doesn't easily change.
Here, your own message in a bottle.
Subject verb object. Evening stalls
in the parking lot, back and forth
a couple of thousand steps
of odd noises and uncertainty.
The rest is anything but silence.
Now at this age still determined
to let song flourish and go where it may.
Once more the brilliant half moon
insisting just so above the treetops
in the south corner of the building.

UNTITLED

I and not I trap light in sound,
a borrowing, a proper theft
before the sun's hung too long.
Like fruit, perhaps, lingering on the branch
or vine, like memory backing up
in its course. Here there, thinking of Ray
plucked at dawn from his reveries.
Too many of us low-hanging fruit
trapped in the ever-easier failing
of song, strands of melody
in the shallows' remaining light.

A full moon along the driveway
following me and not me
just here above the treetops.

EAST WEST

"The sun dies at night," begins
your young man's book, "and when a man dies
he is said to have gone West."
The rest seems disingenuous.
Thinking of you who can help
but recall that those one has loved
must never stop dying with
the rising and falling sun.

Trying so to scribble time
rhyming nevertheless. The sublime
isn't an excuse for a pen
rushing across the page. Why here?
Why now? Filling the emptiness
with a shadow of resolve.
Most excellent and timely shadow
lingering from dawn to dusk.

ZEALOTS FOR LOVE

Is it silence or forgiveness
sounds the hush of darkening night?
Considering the few things
one might remain zealous about.
Twilight walks, morning fog and books,
shelf upon bulging shelf of them.

As for love, a terse disquiet
with the harvest moon looming
fully above me as an answer.

Silences

Proem

A silent abandon around
this desk, outside the window,
in the shimmering hush of palm.
Fragment Science *was a start*
at charting the empty spaces
enlivening our thoughts.
As print shops once included
a technician of white space,
you and I learn to be silent,
listen to our meager pages
mingle with the plentiful sea.
To have come this far, or have we?
To rise with first light and scribble
as colors fill in along the rooftops.

*

No ideas but in the silence
inhabiting things. O green wind
like the greenest rising
from the sea to the southwest.
If one can be said to sleep as far
as recalling what once was possible
or impossible without these words.

*

Which doesn't seem like speaking,
more a ragged memory of words
for worlds recovered in dreams,
a glimpse of a familiar face
slipping just around the corner.
Silence, as Adriano reminds,
is no better than lying,
even when not so easy to ignore.

*

Morning breeze is a wonder,
a thread of hope at the bone
running ahead of my steps.
All a green light glistening
across the hillside, birdsong
widening as day wears on.

*

The ancients sought being in song
rooted in untroubled waters.
You and I must surely begin
as we've begun this far along.
As the trees repeat to us: river
and the river to us: trees.

*

What ideas remain are lost
among the reeds. Pools aswirl
hanging neither upstream nor down,
as the sun slips behind canyon walls
and another night takes its place.
The quiet soon declares all thoughts
privy of thought, all notions
uneasy shifting in the dark.

*

As one might begin once again
at day's end, mostly alone
and surrounded by strangers.
Don't ask what other possibilities
might be, the answer for now
sounds too ominous to consider.

*

In sleep, or at least in my sleep,
the quiet is almost cheerful,
convivial, as with the start
and stop, rising and falling
of a lark's call along the hillside.
A hush across a green stage
adazzle with forgetfulness.

*

Of course the story's older,
more ordinary than you think
when song fills the emptiness.
Forgiven by imagining,
the end surely as the beginning
dragged behind. Thoughts of failure
crown the poplars this morning.

*

The close of a century of dreams,
a finicky liquid of hours undone
by an ever more ruthless intrusion,
skipping a beat or two, alert
for what leads away from the story.
The crack and thud of a car door,
soon a pitter-pattering
and another crack and thud.

*

Past the metal gates over front doors,
the street corners cradling their balls
like rosaries. History's shadow?
Dull words and even duller obsession
in a drowsy current adrift in dreams.
Terse syntax as that night socialism
was once again murdered in sleep.

*

Even backwards and upside-down
or upside-down and backwards,
the cat's definitely invisible
except to the two of us.
The stories aren't very different,
the endings mostly the same.
Unless the beginning sought
is without sound.

*

Pale rose and silver blue of endings,
wisp or two of cloud as night falls.
If hell remains other people,
what then history? A river
flowing toward a silent scream?
What was that animal flashed last night
in the dark below the house?
Silver gray and well past midnight.

www.ingramcontent.com/pod-product-compliance
Lightning Source LLC
Chambersburg PA
CBHW031927080426
42734CB00007B/588